DSC SPEED READS
MANAGEMENT

CW00524669

Flexible Working

Yvonne Perry

Directory of Social Change

In association with:

FARRER&Co

Published by
Directory of Social Change
24 Stephenson Way
London NW1 2DP
Tel. 08450 77 77 07; Fax 020 7391 4804
email publications@dsc.org.uk
www.dsc.org.uk
from whom further copies and a full books catalogue are available.

Directory of Social Change is a Registered Charity no. 800517

First published 2010

ISBN 978 1 906294 06 9

British Library Cataloguing in Publication Data

A catalogue record for this book is available from the British Library

Cover and text designed by Kate Bass
Typeset by Marlinzo Services, Frome
Printed and bound by Martins the Printers, Berwick-upon-Tweed

All Directory of Social Change departments in London:
08450 77 77 07

Directory of Social Change Northern Office:
Research 0151 708 0136

Contents

Introduction

Who will this book help?

The guide will help managers in smaller and medium-sized voluntary organisations to make good flexible working choices for their organisations and staff, and to know their legal responsibilities. It will also help those who are seeking flexible working and wanting guidance on what to expect.

What will it give you?

Flexible working has grown rapidly, driven by economic and social forces. Pressures to cut costs and maximise capital, equipment and people are everywhere. Flexibility for a better balance between personal life and work is now widely accepted. This book covers the different types of flexible working, its pros and cons, the essentials of law and policies, some tips and examples for good practice, and where to find more information and advice.

Chapter 1

What is flexible working?

This chapter describes the main types of flexible working and their suitability for organisations and people.

Flexible working is flexibility of time and place, often described as a working pattern adapted to suit a person's need. Successful flexible working is a marriage of needs – of organisation and individual – to mutual benefit. Flexible working has to comply with working time law, including hours, rest breaks and the working week, as well as health and safety at the place of work. There is a variety of contractual arrangements according to the type of flexible working.

You may have informal flexible working already as a practical solution to staffing problems and individual needs, or the nature of your work may require a particular type of flexible working, such as shifts.

There are many possibilities for flexible working. It can help towards strategic development as well as more effective daily operations. Competitive pressures grip every sector of employment, and flexible working is a powerful tool in dealing with them. Driving down employment and other costs accelerates the use of non-standard working patterns and of space saving practices, such as homeworking and 'hotdesking'.

People may find that the changes open up possibilities and are motivating, provided that they are introduced cooperatively and with sensitivity.

Working hours and times that suit

Part-time work

This is working fewer than normal basic, full-time hours: it is often defined as working fewer than 30 hours a week. The voluntary sector is a major user of this best-known flexible working pattern. Of more than 600,000 workers in the sector, 39% are part-time. Two-thirds are women and nearly half work part-time.

Part-time working helps employers operate for longer hours, cover breaks and peak times, and to keep highly skilled employees who are unable to work full time. Recruiting mothers with young children or older people as part-timers can help if you need to find people with scarce skills. The administration, recruitment and training costs may be higher, as often they are the same for a part-timer as for a full-timer.

There are advantages in fitting work round family, study, leisure or another job. Part-time working is a good example of the trade-off in flexible working between time and money. Research shows that many part-timers are employed below the level of their competence, and that part-time working limits earnings and promotion potential. Also, they can suffer from being wrongly perceived as lacking in commitment, both by managers and colleagues.

Flexitime

Flexitime allows people to choose when to work their hours outside the core times set by the employer. Flexitime helps employers operate over longer periods and provide maximum staff cover in busy hours. It is said to aid staff retention, reduce absenteeism and increase productivity. Employees can feel more in control of their time and workload: they can fit hours around their responsibilities and interests, avoid peak

Top tip

Employees who can choose to work flexibly often reflect this in extra commitment to the organisation rather than less.

Jill Thornton, Personnel Co-ordinator, DSC

travel times and 'bank' some time. For this, effective time recording and trust are essential; manual recording systems can be time-consuming and open to abuse. Time-recording software is often used. Some people feel that flexitime is dated, given the opportunities for flexibility created by information technology (IT) in teleworking and homeworking.

Staggered hours

In this scenario, a workplace has different starting, finishing and break times. This helps the employer to operate for longer working days and accommodate particular staff needs, such as their children's school run.

Compressed working

Employees often like longer blocks of time off, especially without reducing hours and pay: for example, working a nine-day fortnight. It is said to aid recruitment, reduce absence and staff turnover, but it can be harder to organise work and cover, for example in small teams. There are extra costs in keeping premises open longer than necessary. Compressed hours are not suitable for staff working set shift patterns, or where there is no demand for them to be available beyond their normal working hours, such as a 9 to 5 reception desk.

Employees often like longer blocks of time off, especially without reducing hours and pay: for example, working a nine-day fortnight. Travel to work costs may be reduced. However, longer days may not be helpful for some employees, for example those with responsibility for collecting children from childcare or school. In addition, fatigue from longer days may affect employees' performance.

Working more hours or less

Time-off in lieu (TOIL)

This is taking time off to compensate for extra hours worked. Workers have to agree to the practice. It is often used where overtime is not paid: for example, for professional and managerial staff. Time off has to be taken when convenient to the employer. It can be a formal time account arrangement where staff build credits for the extra hours worked. TOIL needs good time recording and trust.

Overtime

Overtime is the extra hours above the basic contracted hours, worked with the employer's agreement, and is widely found with hourly paid staff. When overtime is part of the normal pattern, it is often part of the contract of employment.

Overtime gives employers flexibility for a rapid response to fluctuations in demand, and for 'back of house' work such as maintenance outside normal working time. The costs of recruiting and training extra staff are avoided, although there is extra cost in premium overtime pay rates. Overtime should not be a means of making up for paying badly.

In this scenario, employees earn more but are frustrated when overtime is withdrawn. Consistently long hours may cause fatigue, lower performance and result in unsafe working.

Voluntary reduced time working

An employee can request a voluntary reduction in standard working hours. The employer will base a decision on the practicality of reducing hours to the extent requested and for the time involved. Ensure that staff asking to reduce hours fully understand the effect of pro-rata on pay, pensions and holidays and that your agreement is properly documented.

Zero hours contracts

Contracts do not state the number of hours. Employees tend to be available to work when required and are paid only for the time worked; they may not be paid for waiting time. They should be paid the appropriate hourly rate or the National Minimum Wage while on-call or standby, unless their contracts state otherwise.

In addition, you may come across contracts that guarantee some hours, but do not state regular times when they will be worked.

Working all hours and seasonal peaks

Shift work

This is a pattern of work, usually outside conventional daytime hours, where one employee replaces another on the same job within a 24-hour period.

Some people like shift work: they can have free time when shops and facilities are uncrowded, or they may like regular night work. However, shift work can be detrimental to well-being, such as when it distorts sleep patterns.

Variations of shift organising give workers a greater say, for example:

- shift swapping – staff arrange shifts among themselves to suit their needs according to parameters, ensuring full cover
- self-rostering – this is very similar to shift swapping, where employees schedule their own working day, aiming to accommodate individual preferences as much as possible, to ensure full cover.

Annual hours

In this situation, contracted hours are calculated over a year. The majority are allocated but some are reserved, so staff can be called in at short notice. Annual hours are often used where there is seasonal demand: shift rotas for allocated hours can be organised well in advance so that management and staff can plan ahead. Good supervision is required to use the unallocated hours well, and pay is averaged out over the year. The practice can reduce overtime, the use of temporary staff and encourage teamworking. Although often found in shift work industries, it can be useful elsewhere.

Where next?

For examples of shifts and rotas see Acas, 'Flexible Working and Work–Life Balance': tinyurl.com/ WorkLifeACAS

Where next?

Unite the Union, Amicus *Annualised Hours* guide: tinyurl.com/ AnnualHours

Where next?

For information and case studies about teleworking (and much more), see www.flexibility. co.uk. The Actnow Flex project on teleworking in small and medium-sized businesses may be useful to smaller voluntary organisations: www.flexible-working.org

Top tip

If people work from home, either permanently or temporarily, make sure that everyone knows their contact details.

Flexibility of work location

Teleworking

This is a term used for mostly working away from the office, including homeworking, working on the move, remote working and 'hotdesking'.

Teleworking is widespread but remember that not all jobs lend themselves to teleworking, and not everyone is suited to it or finds it personally beneficial. Managing teleworking successfully is demanding in different ways from managing on-site: it puts more emphasis on measuring performance by output and quality than on attendance. You have to make sure that teleworkers are not isolated or excluded and, if working at home, that their homes can properly accommodate a 'home office' with health and safety, confidentiality and data protection requirements.

Homeworking

Official homeworking is where the main place of work is home. Its advantages include staff retention, high motivation and productivity and reduction in office space requirements. Homeworking also works well for discrete projects and functions.

Employees benefit from:

- saving travel time and costs, or living at a distance
- fitting in family or caring responsibilities (however, it is not a substitute for proper childcare)
- a (hopefully) peaceful working environment.

Working from home on an occasional basis is useful for tasks such as finishing a report. It should not be a soft option.

Flexibility for personal needs

Statutory rights to leave and time off

There are statutory rights (see Chapter 2) to:

- annual holiday
- maternity, paternity and adoption leave
- parental leave
- other special leave.

Term-time working

This is working only in school term times. Permanent or temporary contracts are used; pay is calculated according to the time worked and can be averaged out through the year. The advantages to parents are self-evident. For employers, there may be issues about work cover and organisation.

Jobsharing

A full-time job is split, usually between two people on part-time contracts. Employers may benefit from a wider range of expertise by combining the talents and experience of two people in one job. A jobshare may enable a valued employee to return after maternity leave. If one jobsharer is absent, at least half the work continues and, with agreement, both may work at the same time to cover a peak period. Successful jobshares depend on complementary knowledge, skills and experience and on a good working relationship between the jobsharers.

Sabbaticals/career breaks and secondments

This is an agreed period off, either paid or unpaid. Employers and employees can benefit from a sabbatical by new learning. Employers need to ensure cover and keep the employee informed of important developments. For employees, it can be a refreshing opportunity; secondees gain new insights and experience and can fill a temporary staffing gap.

Phased return to work

Phased return to work is the most common method used to help workers return after sickness, and is used after maternity leave or career breaks. It usually takes

Where next?

CBI/Harvey Nash, *Easing Up?*
CBI/Harvey Nash Employment Trends Survey 2009: tinyurl.com/CBI-Nash

the form of a phased build-up of hours, duties and responsibilities. Alternatively, it may involve home-working, time off for rehabilitation or moving work to easier areas.

Phased retirement and post-65 working

Employees may request flexible working towards a phased retirement: for example, to change hours or work from home all or some of the time, or they might want to apply for a post with less responsibility. Employees could take advantage of 'right to request' legislation to work on beyond 65 or any other retirement age set by the organisation. (However, be aware that the government intends to scrap from October 2011 the so-called default retirement age, which allows employers to dismiss those who are 65 and over on retirement grounds.)

Additional flexibility

Agency workers

Agency workers are taken on: to staff peak periods; to cover absence, leave, unfilled vacancies and freezes on permanent recruitment; or for special projects and skills. For a fee, the agency finds the workers, pays them and handles Pay As You Earn (PAYE) and National Insurance. Workers are provided on an ad hoc, often open-ended, basis. Employers usually require them to be up to speed quickly, but they often need training to use in-house systems and equipment. Some agency workers are highly skilled and experienced, such as IT specialists and interim managers.

Contractors and subcontractors

Contractors are often used, usually for a fixed period, for certain functions: for example, security, or to acquire special skills and experience for a project. Such contractors have a 'contract for services', and may be organisations or individuals. Contractors may

Where next?

Age Discrimination, Y Perry, DSC, 2010.

Top tip

Use an agency you trust: one that knows your organisation and your requirements.

Debra Allcock Tyler, Chief Executive, DSC

subcontract work that they do not carry out themselves but for which they are responsible.

Internships

Although internships (or work experience) are controversial they are popular. They last for a few weeks or months and are part- or full-time. Interns may undertake special projects or a programme of work experience and are paid or given expenses only. A government website, Graduate Talent Pool (graduatetalentpool.direct.gov.uk), aims to match employers and prospective interns.

Internships are a useful additional resource, provided that they are well planned and supervised, the interns are appropriately selected for the task, and they are not substituting for a proper job or taken advantage of pay-wise. Provided that they are genuine volunteers, there is no legal obligation to pay interns the National Minimum Wage, although certain intern rights groups are pressing for this to be changed: for example, see www.internaware.org or www.rightsforinterns.org.uk. (Charities and voluntary organisations may be able to claim exemption in relation to 'voluntary workers' under section 44 of the Minimum Wages Act 1998.)

You may need one or a combination of types of flexible working. There is guidance on the main types of flexible working on the Department for Business, Innovation & Skills and DirectGov websites and at Acas. Other helpful sources include the Working Families website (which has voluntary organisation case studies at: tinyurl.com/WFcasestudies), and www.flexibility. co.uk. The government has an interactive tool to help you choose.

Where next?

BusinessLink, 'Choose the Right Kind of Flexible Working': tinyurl.com/ ChooseRight

Chapter 2

The law and flexible working

This chapter describes the legal implications of flexible working. If you are in doubt, you should seek professional advice.

Many aspects of employment law affect flexible working.

Contracts and employment status

Contract of employment

The contract of employment is a legal agreement, a contract of service between employer and employee. It cannot be changed (varied) without each other's agreement. The contract may be written or oral, but someone employed for more than a month is entitled to a 'written statement' of the most important terms within two months of starting work.

The contract is fundamental in any changes you make. The need to change an employee's place or hours of work due to the introduction of flexible working may be among the reasons for wanting to change a contract of employment. Similarly, an employee may wish to vary their hours or work part time. Contracts of employment can be changed by agreement with the individual or by a collective agreement. The change can be agreed verbally or in writing, but it is better to record it in writing.

Where next?

See the Acas leaflet, 'Varying a Contract of Employment': tinyurl.com/ VaryContract

Agency Workers Regulations 2010: tinyurl.com/ AWR2010

You may have flexibility clauses in employment contracts giving you the right to change certain conditions or a job location. You must not act unreasonably. If the agreed changes alter the terms of an employee's written statement, you must provide an updated written statement showing what has changed within a month of the change.

Employees can insist on changes only if they are covered by a statutory right, such as the 48-hour week. If you wish to change an employment contract you need to consult the employee (or their representative). There will be a breach of contract if you impose a change in contractual terms without the employee's agreement. There are legal requirements on what can be done if you fail to agree.

Employment status

You may have staff on different kinds of contracts and with different employment status. The law makes distinctions between workers, employees and the self-employed. You need to know about these distinctions to be clear about the rights and protections of each category. It is a difficult legal area, so take care. Generally, rights that apply to a 'worker' also apply to an 'employee'. Employees have some additional employment rights. So, in this chapter, references to 'workers' will also relate to employees, whereas references to 'employee' will only cover employees and not extend to workers.

An 'employee' is someone who has entered into, or works under, a contract of employment. 'Worker' is a broader term that includes employees and other groups. A worker is any person who works for you, whether on a contract of employment or any other contract, whereby the individual undertakes to perform work or services personally for another party (normally excluding the self-employed). Workers are entitled to core employment rights and protections, but not unfair dismissal protection and redundancy pay entitlement or maternity, paternity and adoption

Top tip

Relevant factors to determine whether someone is a worker or an employee include: the degree of control exercised by the employer; the exclusivity and duration of the arrangement; the method of payment; etc. If an individual supplies services as part of a business, they will not qualify as a worker.

leave. This is relevant for flexible working because workers are likely to be agency workers, short-term casual workers and some freelancers.

Workers usually have rights:

- to the National Minimum Wage
- to working time limits, including rest breaks, paid holiday and limits on night work
- to protection against unauthorised deductions from pay
- to maternity, paternity and adoption pay
- to protection for part-timers against less favourable treatment
- to Statutory Sick Pay
- to protection for whistleblowers against less favourable treatment
- not to be discriminated against unlawfully.

Employees have all minimum statutory employment rights, including:

- maternity, paternity and adoption leave
- unfair dismissal protection
- Statutory Redundancy Pay
- protection for fixed-term employees from less favourable treatment
- all the rights given to workers.

Establishing employment status can be difficult: it depends on the terms of the contract and the role in the organisation. Tribunals have to look at the facts of each case to see whether a contract of employment is 'implied'. The courts have developed tests to assess this.

Where next?

Citizens Advice Self-Employment Checklist: tinyurl.com/ SEchecklist

Self-employment

A self-employed person does not have a contract of employment, but usually a contract to provide services for a fee within a certain time. Self-employed people have some limited legal protection: for example, not to be discriminated against and to have a safe and healthy working environment on the client's premises. They are responsible for their own tax and National Insurance. You must be clear that anyone whom you regard as self-employed is genuinely so.

Discrimination

Flexible working arrangements must comply with equal pay legislation and anti-discrimination laws on age, disability, gender reassignment, marriage and civil partnership, race, religion or belief, sex and sexual orientation. For example, most part-time workers are women, so an employer could face a claim for sex discrimination by discriminating against part-timers. Much of the Equality Act 2010, which brings together existing discrimination laws, comes into force on 1 October 2010. The EHRC has published guidance documents for employers including one on 'Working hours, flexible working and time off'. There is also corresponding advice for workers.

National Minimum Wage

The National Minimum Wage is a legal right covering almost all workers above compulsory school leaving age. There are different minimum wage rates, increased each October, for the different age groups of workers. Agency workers are normally entitled to receive the National Minimum Wage. Volunteers are excluded, but you should take care (see 'Where next?').

Working time

In general, workers aged over 18 are entitled to:

- 5.6 weeks' (28 days') paid holiday a year (no obligation to give more time off for public holidays)
- work no more than 6 days out of every 7, or 12 out of every 14
- take a 20-minute break if they work more than 6 hours at a stretch – employers are responsible for ensuring that workers are able to take their rest breaks
- work a maximum 48-hour average week – an average week is calculated over a 17-week period, although this may be extended over 26 weeks, for example where 24-hour cover is needed.

Where next?

Good Guide to Employment: Managing and Developing People in Voluntary and Community Organisations, W B Ranken, NCVO, 2010. Equality and Human Rights Commission: www.equality humanrights.com

Where next?

Volunteering England has advice to help you avoid unwittingly making a contract with a volunteer that carries employment rights: tinyurl.com/ volpol

Workers aged 16 and 17 are entitled to:

- take at least 30 minutes' break if they work more than 4.5 hours at a stretch
- work no more than 8 hours a day and 40 hours a week (no averaging)
- have 12 hours' rest between working days and 2 days off every week
- 5.6 weeks' (28 days') holiday a year.

In addition, young workers are entitled not to work between 10pm and 6am (or if it is necessary to work beyond 10pm, between 11pm and 7am).

You may not substitute pay for statutory minimum holiday. All workers are covered by the Working Time Regulations, including part-time, casual, freelance and agency staff. However, there are exceptions: for example the police and emergency services. Workers can agree to work longer than 48 hours a week, provided that they give their agreement in writing, known as an 'opt-out agreement'. Workers whose job enables them to decide how long they work, such as senior managers, are exempt from the limits on average weekly working time and the right to daily and weekly rest breaks. There is employer advice on the government's Businesslink website.

Where next?

Businesslink, 'Policies on Working Time and Time Off': tinyurl.com/ timeoffwork, and 'Working Time and Employment Contracts', tinyurl.com/ EmpContracts

Department for Business, Innovation & Skills, 'Working Time': tinyurl.com/ BISworktime

Contracts for flexibility

Part-time workers

Under the Part-time Workers Regulations 2000, part-time workers are protected against unjustifiably being treated less favourably than a full-time worker on grounds of their part-time status. They should have equality of treatment with full-time workers in respect of their terms and conditions, on a pro-rata basis where appropriate, including in relation to:

- hours
- workload

- pay
- contractual maternity and sick pay
- pensions
- training
- promotion
- holidays.

Overtime is an exception. Part-timers are not entitled to be paid overtime until they have worked more than normal full-time hours. In addition, a very important point is that they must not be treated less favourably in selection for redundancy.

Applying benefits pro-rata can be awkward. For example, holidays may be readily split in proportion but a car cannot be; in this case, it may be possible to work out a financial equivalent. An employer has to be able to justify withholding a benefit from a part-timer.

An employer has to show a solid reason, called an *objective justification*, for unfavourable treatment: that it was necessary and appropriate to achieving a legitimate aim, such as a genuine business objective.

Temporary staff

Employees need a minimum period of continuous employment with their employer to qualify for various employment rights such as protection from unfair dismissal after one year's service. Many temporary workers do not build up sufficient service; however, their rights from day one do include protection against discrimination and a safe place to work. Temporary staff are likely to fall into other categories of worker – for example, fixed-term workers or agency staff – and so will be covered by the legislation protecting each group.

Fixed-term contracts

A fixed-term contract is one that ends at an agreed point.

Top tip

Fair dismissal must be for a potentially fair reason as set out in law. Non-renewal of a fixed-term contract will often be potentially fair due to redundancy, but this relates to the relevant facts of the case including, for example, the reason for using a fixed-term contract or the employee's performance. Establish which reason you intend to rely on before the contract expires and follow a fair procedure.

Termination of employment through the expiry of a fixed-term contract is regarded as a dismissal in law and is subject to the law of unfair dismissal. You must not treat fixed-term contract employees less favourably than permanent staff doing comparable work without objective justification. The Fixed Term Employees (Prevention of Less Favourable Treatment) Regulations 2002 give fixed-term contract employees the right:

- to statutory redundancy payments after two years' service;
- to claim unfair dismissal after one year; and
- to the position becoming permanent, if the fixed-term contract lasts for more than four years (see tinyurl.com/fixedtermcontract).

Pro-rata and objective justification rules also apply to fixed-term contracts, but with a difference. Employers can pay fixed-term employees at a higher rate than permanent employees, instead of providing them with the same benefits as other employees.

Agency workers

Agency workers are engaged by an employment business to perform work for one or more of that business's clients. They have either a contract for services with the agency or, less often, a contract of employment. This determines employment rights (see 'Employment Status', p. 15). Agency workers have protection from discrimination and harassment by both agency and client, and have whistleblowing protection. Along with the agency, employers have health and safety responsibilities to agency workers and for ensuring compliance with other rules: for example, rest periods under working time law.

The Agency Workers Regulations 2010 will come into force on 1 October 2011, now subject to further government consideration. The new law will extend 'equal treatment' to agency workers: that is, that their basic working and employment conditions (pay,

Top tip

Legal note: Agency workers can become an employee or a worker of the employment business or its client, in which case the agency worker will have all the usual rights of an employee or worker against that party.

working hours, overtime, breaks, rest periods, holidays and access to training and collective facilities such as childcare) should be at least the same as if the agency worker had been recruited directly to do the same job. Some provisions will apply when the agency worker has been working in the same role with the same hirer for 12 continuous calendar weeks, during one or more assignments. Others will apply from the start of the engagement.

Paid and unpaid time off

Statutory Sick Pay

Statutory Sick Pay (SSP) replaces earnings for staff who are sick. For more information see tinyurl.com/statsickpay. Record-keeping is important and SSP can be complicated to work out for people with varied work patterns.

Maternity, paternity and adoption leave and pay

Pregnant women can take time off for antenatal appointments (for employees, this is paid; for workers, this is unpaid).

All pregnant employees are entitled to a total of 52 weeks' maternity leave. Statutory Maternity Pay is paid for 39 weeks. There is a length of service period and earnings qualification for maternity pay. Workers on a contract for services do not have a right to maternity leave, but if they qualify as 'employed earners' for National Insurance purposes, they may be entitled to maternity pay. Employers can reclaim all or most Statutory Maternity Pay from the government. Women who are not eligible for maternity pay may be entitled to a government benefit – the Maternity Allowance.

A similar approach is taken in the provisions for adoption and paternity leave. Employees are entitled to leave and pay (also subject to service and earnings conditions). Workers are not entitled to leave, but may be to pay.

Where next?

HM Revenue & Customs, 'Maternity, paternity, adoption, sickness': tinyurl.com/HMRC-MPAS

Additional Paternity Leave Regulations 2010: tinyurl.com/PatLeave2010

Top tip

Where employers provide a contractual right to enhanced maternity pay, this will be in addition to Statutory Maternity Pay, although any additional pay will not be recoverable from the government.

Margaret Lloyd, Director, Walking with Leaders Ltd

Note that new measures were introduced on 6 April 2010 for additional paternity leave and pay. It will apply where children are due on or after 3 April 2011. The practical effect is to enable a mother who has returned to work without using her full statutory maternity leave entitlement to transfer the second six months of maternity leave to the father.

Where next?

Businesslink, 'Parental Leave and Time Off for Dependants': tinyurl.com/ ParDepLeave

Parental leave

Employees with at least a year's service can take up to 13 weeks' unpaid leave for each child (born or adopted) for whom they are responsible, and will use the leave in a block or split, up to the child's fifth birthday. Employees with disabled children can take up to 18 weeks' unpaid leave up to the eighteenth birthday.

Other time off

Time off rights for employees that are relevant to flexible working include:

Where next?

Businesslink, 'New Right for Employees to Request Time to Train': tinyurl.com/ time2train.

The Age and Employment Network (TAEN), 'New Right to Request Time Off for Training': tinyurl.com/ TimeOffTAEN

- a reasonable period off, unpaid, for an emergency affecting a dependant
- reasonable unpaid time off for public duties: for example a magistrate or school governor
- the right to request time off for special festivals or spiritual observance days – there is no statutory obligation to grant such leave, but you risk discrimination if you do not.

For 16 to 17-year-old employees with few or no qualifications, reasonable paid time off for study or training is allowed to help improve future employment prospects. Employees at 18 years old can take reasonable paid time off before their nineteenth birthday to finish any qualifications in progress.

From 6 April 2010, employees in organisations with more than 250 employees have a right to request time off for study or training to improve an employee's own effectiveness in the business, or to improve the effectiveness of the business (for example, to use new software). The new right will extend to employees of *all* employers on 6 April 2011 (although this is now subject to a new government consultation).

Employers must allow time off for jury service. They do not have to pay, but the juror can claim for travel, subsistence and loss of earnings. Employees are protected against unfair treatment due to selection for jury service.

Health, safety and other obligations

Health and safety

Employers owe employees statutory duties in respect of health and safety. Independent contractors may not be covered by these duties, although they will be covered by employers' common law duty of care regarding occupier's liability.

Employers have a general duty to provide a safe working environment as far as is reasonably practicable. Health and safety at work legislation applies whether employees are working in a conventional office or remotely.

Employees also must take reasonable care of their own health and safety and that of anyone else who might be affected by what they do. An employee is responsible for reporting all employment-related hazards to their own or others' health.

Employers are required to do a risk assessment of all work activities carried out by their workers, including those working from home or elsewhere. Homeworkers should carry out a self-assessment of the risks from their work in the home.

Assessments should identify the hazards and then assess the extent of the risks, for example from electrical or computer equipment. Employers are responsible for:

Where next?

The Health and Safety Executive (HSE) Fatigue/Risk Index tinyurl.com/ RiskIndex

Managing Shiftwork guide (HSG 256): tinyurl.com/ shiftworkHSE

Top tip

The Data Protection Act 1998 provides for how and when personal data can and should lawfully be processed. Employers must observe data protection obligations regarding current and former job applicants; employees; agency, contract and other casual workers; and sometimes volunteers such as those on work experience. Duties under the Act apply at every stage of the employment relationship, from recruitment to even after the termination.

- the safety of equipment and its suitability
- checking safety compliance
- providing necessary training
- First Aid provision for the homeworker.

There is no specific health and safety legislation on shift work, but employers' duty of care for their employees and others includes removing or controlling the risks of tiredness by good shift work planning and organising. Employers have a responsibility for the health and safety of others such as the public, who might be affected by their activities, which is why it is important to control aspects such as fatigue.

There are special night working provisions under working time law. The normal working hours of a night worker should not exceed eight hours in any 24-hour period. The required daily or weekly rest periods can be excluded for shift workers to cover the changing of shifts, but compensatory rest must be provided.

Data protection

Employers are responsible for taking steps to ensure the protection of data used and processed by on-site or off-site workers for professional purposes. There are at least three separate situations relevant to flexible working, of which the employer ought to be aware:

- self-employed and with the office at home
- employed by an organisation and based at home
- employed by an organisation and based in an office, but taking work home regularly or occasionally.

Chapter 3

Requesting flexible working

This chapter covers the rights of parents and carers to request flexible working. Entitlement, procedure, eligibility and timescale are outlined.

The right to request flexible working

Anyone may ask to work flexibly, but not everyone has a legal right to have their request considered seriously. Here, the guide focuses on the legal 'right to request' flexible working by employees with parental and caring responsibilities. The right is to ask for flexibility, but not a right to work flexibly. For example, employees can ask to change their hours, times and place of work (home or business). However, the story may not end there. The Coalition Document states, 'we will extend the right to request flexible working to all employees...' (*The Coalition: our Programme for Government*, © Crown copyright, 2010, p. 18)

Employer's responsibility to consider requests

You have a duty to consider requests seriously and show good reason if you reject them. There may be circumstances when you are unable to accept a request (see 'Grounds for refusal', p. 27).

Where next?

Carers UK, *Carers and Employment: a Guide to the Right to Request Flexible Working*: tinyurl.com/ FlexWorkR2R

Eligibility

Eligible

Employees who are, or expect to:

- be parents* of children under 17
- be parents of disabled children under 18 in receipt of Disability Allowance
- be responsible for the child's upbringing and be making an application in order to care for the child
- be carers** of an adult – that is, over 18
- have worked for you for 26 weeks continuously before applying
- have not made another application to work flexibly during the past 12 months, even if for a different kind of care – for example, an adult instead of a child.

Not eligible

- agency workers
- self-employed contractors
- members of the armed services
- employees who do not fit the statutory eligibility criteria

*The employee must be the mother, father, adopter or foster parent or guardian, or be married to or the partner or civil partner of one of these.

** The person needing care must be married to or partner, civil partner or close relative of the employee, or be living at the same address. There is no definition of care, but it is likely to involve personal care and domestic tasks.

Where next?

Acas booklet:
The Right to Apply for Flexible Working: a Short Guide for Employers, Working Parents and Carers:
tinyurl.com/ right2apply

Procedure

Both employee and employer have to follow a highly prescriptive procedure, unless they come to an arrangement informally. Where an appeal is involved, an application can take three months from receipt by the employer to the final decision. Many successful requests are dealt with informally. The government has model letters and forms for use by employees and employers at each stage.

In the event of a final rejection the employee may: seek informal discussion; use the grievance procedure; seek experienced help such as from a union representative; seek Acas information or conciliation, or if no solution is found refer to the Acas Arbitration Scheme; complain to an employment tribunal.

Timeline for requests*

Application received
⇩
Meeting to discuss application within 28 days
⇩
Employer writes with decision within 14 days ⇨ Acceptance
⇩
Rejection
⇩
Will employee appeal? If yes, they must write, setting out their case, within 14 days
⇩
Meeting to discuss appeal within 14 days
⇩
Employer writes with decision within 14 days ⇨ Acceptance
⇩
Rejection

* The time limits can be extended by mutual agreement.
Source: Department for Business, Innovation & Skills

Grounds for refusal

- Employee is not eligible or has failed to follow correct procedure
- Structural changes
- Additional costs
- Negative impact on quality, performance or customer service
- Cannot reorganise work among other staff
- Lack of work when the employee wants to work

Contract changes

A new work pattern agreed via the formal legal route will be a contractual variation to the employee's employment and permanent, unless a further agreement is reached mutually. Imposing a unilateral change to an employee's contractual terms will amount to a breach of contract. Always mutually agree any trial period and put anything agreed in writing.

Top tip

There is a danger that an employee whose request has been rejected could seek redress via a sex discrimination claim (no limit on compensation). Take particular care with requests from returners from maternity leave.

Margaret Lloyd, Director, Walking with Leaders Ltd

Where next?

Flexible working forms for employees: www. bis.gov.uk

Template letters to apply and respond to requests for flexible working: Directgov, 'Flexible Working: Making an Application': tinyurl.com/FWapp

Businesslink, 'Choosing the Right Type of Flexible Working': tinyurl.com/ RightType

Chapter 4

Managing flexible working

The chapter gives advice on adopting a flexible working policy. It covers practical, managing and operational concerns and potential benefits.

Why a policy is valuable

Your interest in flexible working may be because:

- your kind of work demands it – for example, shift working
- you need to explore additional types of flexible working patterns
- you have to find ways of being more cost-effective, raising standards, improving service delivery and making better use of resources
- you need to improve staff morale and commitment, or reduce absence
- you are receiving requests for flexible working
- you need to comply with the 'right to request' law
- you cannot recruit or retain sought-after skills and staff unless you offer flexible working options
- applicants and present staff expect it
- you think that it is increasingly the way of the working world – the way to go.

Case study

Our flexible working practices are good for the organisation and good for the staff, so it's a win-win situation. We know we can call on staff to put extra hours in when the business needs it, because they know they'll be able to get the time back via flexi-leave. All staff have a remote connection set up on their PC, so they can work from home if necessary. This has been particularly useful when people have had swine flu – we couldn't have them back in the office because they were still infectious, but they felt well and able to work, and didn't want to come back to the backlog they knew was piling up. So they worked from home.

Philip Baker, Personnel Manager, EIRIS

Quite apart from legal compliance, the process of establishing a formal policy will help you make your choices: it will be your stated commitment to the principles and practice of flexible working. Your perceptions of the advantages and practicalities of flexible working are important, and so is an open mind. Trust is fundamental to successful flexible working.

Key features of a policy

Many policies are simply based on the entitlements and procedure of the 'right to request' law. Others extend flexible working beyond the basic law, such as extending the right to all employees who have worked for the organisation for 26 weeks. Essentially, the policy needs to state:

- your commitment to flexible working and what the policy is designed to achieve
- who is eligible

Top tip

If you wish to change an existing flexible working policy that is contractual – that is, part of the contract of employment – you need to agree the changes (see Contracts of employment, p. 14).

'Assume any role can be done flexibly, providing it is not to the detriment of the business.'

Opportunity Now: tinyurl.com/ OppNow

Where next?

For an in-depth study of the impact of flexible working practices on employee performance that shows many positive features, see: 'Flexible Working and Performance', Working Families and Cranfield School of Management, tinyurl.com/ WorkFam

- options for and descriptions of types of flexible working, and where to find more detail and procedures
- the procedure for applications
- the method of monitoring
- the date of policy review
- the name of the staff member or department responsible for the policy.

Devising the policy

Checklist

❏ Make a senior manager accountable for setting up and implementing the policy.

❏ Devise the policy jointly: for example, with a multi-level, cross-departmental project team.

❏ Analyse the effects of types of flexible working on strategy, operations, customer service, staffing levels, supervision, communication and consultation.

❏ Assess which jobs are suitable for flexible working (Acas has a suitability questionnaire: see: tinyurl.com/AcasQuestionnaire).

❏ Decide who will deal with applications, take meetings and appeals and handle administration.

❏ Plan ahead, consult widely and trial proposals.

❏ Decide how you will roll out the policy.

❏ Set a review date.

Putting policy into practice

Checklist

❏ Advertise and communicate the policy: for example, by briefing meetings, producing newsletters, using the intranet.

❏ Issue guidance for managers.

- ❏ Train managers in particular kinds of flexible working that are new to them. Many managers are not used to managing people who have some choice about when or where they work, whom they cannot see at work, or where the employer's responsibilities, such as for health and safety, extend beyond the office.

- ❏ Train staff for different roles where they may need to cover.

- ❏ Ensure that the rest of the team are clear on when people are or are not working. Clearly indicate this in diaries. Make sure that expectations are realistic of how flexible working will work and impact teams upfront.

- ❏ Make sure that your IT department will support and keep up with flexible working developments.

- ❏ Review the criteria for performance. Is there too much weight on attendance and not enough on quality and output?

- ❏ Measure performance for evidence of the positive effects of flexible working on performance and commitment, and to substantiate the business case.

- ❏ Measure take-up to monitor progress.

- ❏ Include questions about flexible working in staff surveys.

- ❏ Review other policies. Do they support flexible working, or deter it by being based on the notion of a full-time 'always visible' employee?

> **Top tip**
>
> Make staff aware of the realities of maintaining continuity and still being part of the team. There comes a point when you simply cannot keep reducing hours.
>
> **Sue Livett, Managing Director, Aldingbourne Trust**

Some challenges

Flexible working takes time to bed down and you will meet numerous challenges, not least in how to be flexible with staff. For example in a care environment, some staff may want to reduce their hours so much that they cannot realistically continue to be a key worker. They may need to spend so much time catching up on staff meeting notes, journals, communication, supervision and training that they will not have time for meaningful hands-on work.

Top tip

'Our policies have meant that we have avoided spending the £1.5 million it would cost to build the new office we would need if our expanding workforce all worked 9am to 5pm, Monday to Friday.'

Ahsan Khan, CEO, Loreburn Housing Association (in *The Way Ahead*, Investors in People Scotland, issue 4, December/January 2006, p. 6)

There is a danger in setting precedents: if staff say that they cannot work weekends, or do not want to do sleep-in shifts, this can cause difficulties with the rest of the team. Above all, in such circumstances it is essential to consider the needs of the project and see how flexible you can be until the hours just do not fit into the demands of the job.

Other challenges include the following:

- initial scepticism about employees' timekeeping, commitment and productivity – managers have to make efforts to value quality of work and output, to communicate differently, and rethink teamworking
- flexible working requires a high calibre of supervision
- staff may be wary, preferring informal arrangements in case they jeopardise career prospects by making a formal request
- informal arrangements can be abused and formal training needs overlooked
- take-up of flexible working may be disappointing because staff are unaware of their options
- there is evidence that flexible workers may not be chosen for important or urgent projects because they are not visible or not working full time
- some flexible working runs the risk of staff feeling isolated or left out of the communication loop – at the same time, flexible workers become very conscious of how they spend time, so they resent wasting it at meetings they regard as unproductive (even if you think them important)
- it may be difficult to accommodate different simultaneous requests
- part-timers may be working for longer to squeeze an almost full-time job into part-time hours
- the boundaries between work and home can merge detrimentally.